FRANCISCO PIZARRO

Conquistador of the Attack on Peru

Written by Aude Cirier
In collaboration with Marc Malevez
Translated by Jessica Foster

History   50MINUTES.com

FRANCISCO PIZARRO

KEY INFORMATION

- **Born:** around 1478 in Trujillo (Crown of Castile).
- **Died:** 26 June 1541 in Lima (Peru).
- **Aim of the expedition:** conquering Peru.
- **Regions of the world he explored:** the Antilles, followed by Central and South America.
- **Famous discoveries:** Peru and the Inca Empire.

INTRODUCTION

Francisco Pizarro was one of the key figures of Spanish colonisation. After taking part in several exploration expeditions to South America, Pizarro landed on the West coast and discovered the Inca Empire, whose prosperity and wealth had already been the subject of mythical tales. After two heroic attempts, in 1529 the Spanish monarchy granted him the necessary permission and privileges to set off on a colonisation expedition to Peru with two associates. Motivated by unlimited ambition and an incredible will, Pizarro overcame all the obstacles to successfully complete his expedition: combining diplomacy, strategy and power play – sometimes at the cost of inconceivable violence – he successfully defeated the main Inca leaders and Spanish hopefuls for power in Peru. He captured the then capital, Cuzco, in 1533, and founded new Spanish towns throughout his expedition, including Lima (Ciudad de los Reyes) in 1535.

With his discovery of the Inca Empire and its wealth, Pizarro laid the bases of a new colonial state across which his family wished to assert its control, with the support of the Spanish monarchy and to the detriment of the other conquistadors. Although colonisation was carried out using violence against indigenous populations who put up real resistance, greed, jealousy and desire led to a civil war which destroyed the Spanish troops, up to the highest ranks: in June 1541, Pizarro was fatally attacked by supporters of his former associate, Almagro (1475-1538), whom he had had executed.

BIOGRAPHY

Portrait of Francisco Pizarro.

The illegitimate son of a noble captain, Gonzalo Pizarro y
Rodríguez de Aguilar (1446-1522), and a servant girl from a
poor family, Francisca González, Francisco Pizarro was the

eldest child of many siblings, more illegitimate than legitimate. Little is known about his early years. The date of birth 16 March 1478, which is sometimes assigned to him, has not been confirmed. Kept away from the family by his father (whose last will and testament he moreover did not feature in), Pizarro was raised in extremely humble circumstances by his mother and was never educated. As he was illiterate, he welcomed a career in the armed forces. We know that he was in Seville in 1493, then in Italy from 1495 to 1498.

From February 1502 onwards, sources allow us to trace his life more accurately: he set sail with 2500 men for Hispaniola (modern-day Haiti/Dominican Republic), under the command of Nicolás de Ovando (1460-1518), Governor of the Indies. He was opportunistic and took part in as many expeditions as possible. In 1509, he went with Alonso de Ojeda (c. 1468-1515) to colonise the Columbian coast and the Gulf of Urabá. He then joined Martín Fernández de Enciso (c. 1470-1528), with whom he founded the town of Santa María la Antigua del Darién, capital of the Province of Tierra Firme (now in the municipality of Unguía, Colombia). When the conquistador Vasco Núñez de Balboa (1475-1519) led an uprising there which resulted in the overthrow of Enciso, Pizarro became his lieutenant and right-hand man. Together, on 29 September 1513, they reached the Pacific Ocean after crossing the Isthmus of Panama. Between 1514 and 1519, Pizarro was the lieutenant of the new governor, Pedrarias Dávila (1468-1531), the instigator of several expeditions aimed at bringing back gold and slaves. Pizarro first won his spurs during the confrontation between Dávila and Núñez de Balboa. Demonstrating infallible loyalty towards the governor, he had his former superior arrested and executed and was rewarded. Having made a name for himself, he became one of the founders and public figures of the city of Panama in August 1519.

The portrait of a man full of good intentions

The Spanish historian Gonzalo Fernández de Oviedo y Valdés (1478-1557), who worked at the government of Darién, thus describes Pizarro: "A good man with a good mind, a strong build, neither the character nor the education of a governor [...], who behaves in a measured way, seems full of good intentions although he does not say much, and is already well-known for his courage"[1] (1885: 144-147).

At the beginning of the 1520s, Pizarro embarked on new discoveries. With two associates, he set out on the conquest of the south, thus inextricably linking his personal history to that of Peru. This was attested by the birth of his two children from his marriage (in the Inca rite) to the daughter of the Sapa Inca Huayna Capac (ruler c. 1493-1528), Inés Yupanqui (whose real name was Quispe Sisa, c. 1516-1559): Francisca (1534-1598), who was the first mixed-race child of Spanish and Peruvian heritage and embodied the union of the two nations, while Gonzalo, who was born the following year, died young (1546). Pizarro was a symbol of conquistador

---

1. This quotation has been translated by 50Minutes.com.

power and its consequences, and was assassinated on
26 June 1541 in Lima.

CONTEXT

RIVALRY SURROUNDING THE DISCOVERY OF NEW WORLDS

After the first voyage of Christopher Columbus (Genoese explorer, 1451-1506) to The Bahamas in 1492, exploration expeditions rapidly increased in number: in 1497, Vasco da Gama (Portuguese explorer, c. 1469-1524) reached the Cape of Good Hope and revealed a new way to access the East Indies; Pedro Álvares Cabral (Portuguese explorer, c. 1460-1520) discovered Brazil in 1500; and Hernandez de Cordoba (Spanish explorer, c. 1475-1517) travelled the length of the coasts of Yucatán in 1517. Ferdinand Magellan (Portuguese explorer, 1480-1521) launched his expedition in 1519, while Hernán Cortés (Spanish conquistador, 1485-1547) discovered Mexico in the same year. Pedro de Alvarado (Spanish conquistador, c. 1485-1541) founded Santiago de Guatemala in 1525.

As well as his position in the military, Pizarro undertook various trade and mining activities and became an associate of another conquistador, Diego de Almagro (c. 1480-1538). It was undoubtedly Cortés's resounding success and the discovery of the Aztec Empire in November 1519 that triggered this enterprise.

Helped along in their mission by favourable conditions, Pizarro and Almagro took advantage of the imperial policies of Charles V (1500-1558), who wanted to assert Spanish power over everything valuable that the discovery and conquest of America could provide. A land of wealth and illusions, America kindled much greed and desire, attracting those who aspired to glory.

FIRST ATTEMPTS AND FAILURES

First expedition (November 1524-mid-1525)

In 1524, Pizarro and Almagro partnered with an Andalusian priest, Hernando de Luque (died in 1532), and founded the *Empresa del Levante*, whose aim was clear: the discovery and conquest of the south.

According to historians, after the three men agreed their commitments to one another during a ceremony that took place in May 1524, they started to prepare for their first expedition: Pizarro left Panama in mid-November with 110 men and two fairly unstable ships. The largest ship, the *Santiago*, was only a handmade caravel; the other was in a poor state. Having passed Taboga Island (Gulf of Panama), then the Pearl Islands, they first disembarked in a place they named Puerto Piña. They then ventured inland in the hopes of finding indigenous people and food, in vain. Each time they landed somewhere, the same scenario played out and the expedition turned into a disaster: a hostile environment and difficult access conditions deterred the Spanish mission before they could find what they were looking for. Near the mouth of a river that they named the Río de la Espera ('River of Waiting'), Pizarro and his men found respite and food in an abandoned indigenous fort. They then ransacked several of the surrounding villages. The Native Peruvians retaliated and injured the Spanish leader with heavy arrow fire. Left for dead, Pizarro regained consciousness and agreed to his men's insistent requests to return to Panama. They stopped in Chochama, in south-east Panama, where Almagro came to their aid on board the *San Cristobal*, after nearly losing his life in the same location as his associate.

Second expedition (January 1526-March 1528)

While Pizarro stayed in Chochama, Almagro tried to convince the governor Pedrarias Dávila to get a new expedition underway, as the first had already cost many lives and a large amount of money. Officially appointed head of this second expedition, Almagro left for Chochama at the end of 1525 with the *Santiago* and the *San Cristobal*, a few small landing boats, 110 soldiers, a few horses, slaves and weapons. His main objective was to reach the Río de la Espera and the fortress where both he and Pizarro had nearly died. By way of revenge, the Spanish men destroyed the Native Peruvians who had settled there, demonstrating all their determination, before setting off again towards the south. In each Native Peruvian village, Pizarro and his men attacked the natives and retaliated violently. Beyond the San Juan River, an entirely new horizon was opening itself up to them. They confronted the Native Peruvians, stole their gold and took prisoners for the slave market in Panama. The increasing conflicts were violently repressed.

On Magdalena Island, Pizarro set up a camp from where he could launch his expedition to the south. Faced with problems with supplies and the natives' hostility, he was forced to send Almagro to Panama on board the *Santiago* to seek reinforcements and provisions. There, Almagro received the support of the new governor, Pedro de los Ríos (died in 1547), and the confirmation of the titles granted by his predecessor. Almagro recruited around 40 men from Spain, bought horses, equipment, food and other essentials, and left for San Juan again at the beginning of 1527. During this time, the *San Cristobal*, under the command of the explorer Bartolomeo Ruiz de Estrada (1482-1532) paved the way and reached the north coast of Ecuador. His fortunate encounter with a small boat carrying gold and silver objects, as well as necklaces made of pearls and precious stones, was tangible proof that a rich civilisation must be located not far from there.

When Almagro returned, the two ships set sail again towards Gallo Island (in Tumaco Bay, in the south of modern-day Colombia), passed the mouth of the Esmeraldas River and travelled along the coast of Ecuador. Underpinned by exhaustion and disillusionment, a violent disagreement broke out between the two associates, who argued about how to manage operations and troops. While they were stopped on Gallo Island between June and August 1527, Pizarro sent Almagro back to Panama with a letter for the governor in order to get reinforcements, luring them in with the promise of new lands that were about to be discovered. Aware of and concerned about the human and financial costs, Pedro de los Ríos sent the captain Juan Tafur not only to bring back the men who wanted to return, but to put an end to the expedition. According to legend, Pizarro left the choice up to his men, drawing a line in the sand that they were free to cross (which would mean that they were staying by their leader's side) or not. Only 13 men – known as

Los Trece de la Fama ('The Famous Thirteen') – are reported to have crossed it. They were then joined by Ruiz de Estrada, whom Pedro de los Ríos, who was in difficulty in Panama, had finally authorised to leave for six months, after which everyone would have to return and report on their discoveries. Thus, after several weeks of sailing, and accompanied by Native Peruvians, discoveries started pouring in: Tumbes, Paita, Isla Foca, Lobos de Tierra and many others. Each time, the Spaniards received a warm welcome, enabling them to seize the lands easily. After searching in vain for the town of Chincha that the natives in Tumbes had extensively praised, Pizarro set off again for Panama, which he reached in March 1528, and where he was received with honours. The route had been mapped out: the conquest could begin.

THE CONQUEST OF PERU

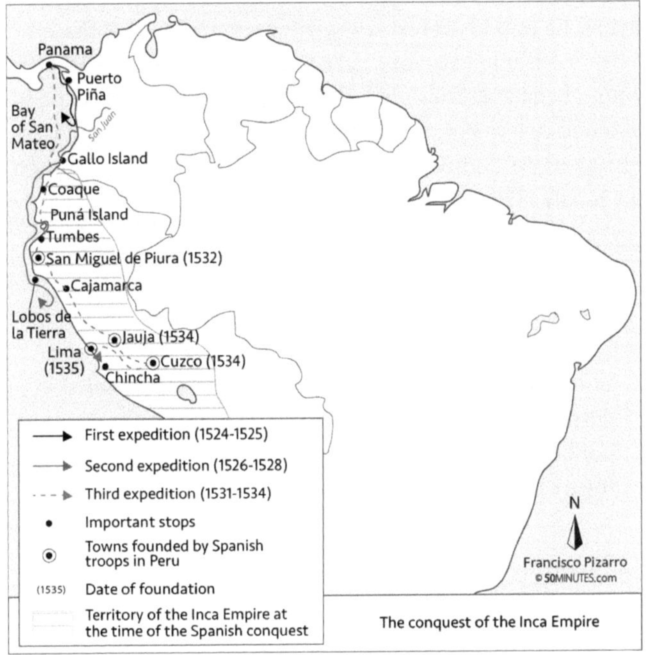

The conquest of the Inca Empire

CAPITULACIÓN DE TOLEDO (26 JULY 1529)

Empowered by his success, Pizarro thought he could easily organise the conquest of new lands. However, as the human and financial costs of the first two expeditions were blamed on him, he was forced to go to the king for the money and permission needed to organise a new mission. Accompanied by exotic species and a few natives, and assisted by Diego del Corral – a jurist who specialised in negotiations – Pizarro reached Seville at the end of 1528. But the welcome there was far from what he expected: thrown in prison because of debts, he and his travel companions were freed at the emperor's order in February 1529. Pizarro then went to Toledo, where he found Charles V. The emperor was impressed and listened to him but, forced to leave for Italy, left his advisers to negotiate and write the *Capitulación*, which was signed on 26 July 1529.

THE *CAPITULACIÓN*

The *Capitulación* was a contract drawn up between the explorers and the monarchy. Its clauses specified the domains in which each of them held power, and the honours and economic consequences for them and future immigrants.

The privileges that were set out in 1529 were essentially of benefit to Pizarro. Indeed, he was authorised to continue with the discovery and conquest of Peru – across a distance of around 700 miles, from the Santiago River to the region of Chincha – he was appointed Governor and Captain General of Peru, and was paid twice as much as his associate. Additionally, he took on various functions such as *adelandato* (judiciary officer with a mandate over a jurisdiction) and *alguacil mayor* (officer in charge of police and security). He also successfully sought the right to build four fortresses of which he would be the governor, and to assign land and terrain to build on to the Spaniards. To manage this new province, he notably had to appoint and pay an *alcade mayor* (chief magistrate), ten knights, thirty foot soldiers, a doctor and an apothecary.

His associates from the *Empresa del Levante* received fewer bonuses, which would be at the origin of their rivalry. Hernando de Luque was appointed universal protector of all the Native Peruvians in the province, despite having expected to be appointed Bishop of Tumbes, while Diego de Almagro, promoted to the status of hidalgo (noble gentleman) – a slight consolation – was only appointed Governor of Tumbes, with an annual salary. As for the other men in the crew, including the sailor Ruiz de Estrada, promoted to *piloto mayor*, and the Famous Thirteen, they were notably awarded honorary titles, promotions and payment. The charter also stipulated fiscal advantages for the new immigrants to come, as it was clearly stated that discovery was not the expedition's only aim: the monarchy was also counting on their populating and exploiting new lands, and Pizarro had six months to launch his expedition.

A FAMILY AFFAIR

When he set sail from Seville for Panama, Pizarro was accompanied by several of his half-brothers whom he had met during the journey: Hernando Pizarro (c. 1500-1578), the only legitimate child of all his siblings, whom he would put in charge of the political and economic negotiations with the monarchy; Juan (1511-1536), and Gonzalo (c. 1502-1548), two illegitimate half-brothers. The former would die in Cuzco in 1536 and the latter would play an important role during the conquest of Peru, then, following Francisco's death, would become the leader of a rebellion against the monarchy. Finally, a fourth (this time on his mother's side), Francisco Martín de Alcantára (c. 1500-1541), to whom Pizarro would become extremely close, also joined the expedition.

In Seville in autumn 1529, there were around 150 men taking part in the expedition, on board four ships. Pizarro set a course for Nombre de Dios, the port of the isthmus, on the Atlantic coast. When he arrived, in March or April 1530, he encountered Almagro, who was unhappy with the fact that the *Capitulación* granted Pizarro a disproportionately large share, thinking that he was disregarding the work of his associates and men, and did not hesitate to tell him this. The presence of Pizarro's brothers, whom historians have described as 'inflated' with pride, managed to stir up tensions. When Almagro threated to launch a simultaneous expedition, Pizarro gave in on some points, such as the fair sharing of all the wealth Peru had to offer among the three associates.

THE RESULT OF FIERCE AMBITION

On 30 January 1531, the expedition left the port of Panama with the aim of conquering territories.

In February, the fleet landed in the bay of San Mateo, near the mouth of the Esmeraldas River. The 180 men under the command of Hernando and Juan Pizarro set off and acclimatised to the environment. From there, their progression along the south-west coast unfolded without a hitch: from Atacames, they travelled to Cancebi (the first 'pacified' village), then to the Cojimíes region. From February to October, the troops set up in Coaque, whose inhabitants had fled inland when they saw the Spanish fleet arriving, abandoning their riches. As well as increasingly frequent tensions with the Native Peruvians, the men of the expedition endured difficult living conditions. Reinforcements arrived, led by Sebastián de Benalcázar (1480-1551), a charismatic character and friend of Pizarro, who led the cavalry and strategically placed some of his men in key positions, with the main aim of limiting the Pizarro brothers' influence. In November, the expedition reached the most westerly point of Ecuador (modern-day Santa Elena), before reaching Puná Island at the end of the month.

Welcomed on 30 November by Tumbalá, the king of the island, Pizarro was allowed by him to explore the territory. Despite this warm welcome, Pizarro felt some mistrust towards the Native Peruvian king, and took advantage of the rivalry between Tumbalá and the Native Peruvians in Tumbes (placed under Almagro's authority following the *Capitulación*) to arrest the king following his first misde-meanour and deliver him to his enemies. The latter had him decapitated, inciting the uprising of the island's villagers. The conflicts, during which Hernando Pizarro was injured, were extremely violent. For Pizarro, the lesson was clear: it was necessary to divide the Native Peruvians to assert control. At the same time, two ships arrived, loaded with supplies and reinforcements from Nicaragua. They had been chartered by Pizarro himself and were under the command of Hernando de Soto (c. 1496-1542), one of the main captains of the conquest of Nicaragua.

The land conquest of Peru, for which Pizarro was counting on his alliance with the people of Tumbes and their leader Chilimasa, could now be launched from Puná Island. It started in April 1532, but the disappointments soon began to flow: on the way, Native Peruvians betrayed the conquistadors, stealing many of the riches and killing or injuring many of their travel companions.

When he arrived in Tumbes, Pizarro forced Chilimasa and his men to follow him, in exchange for their lives. Leaving behind heavy goods, injured men and royal officers in Tumbes, Pizarro began an expedition along a route that had recently been discovered by Francisco Martín de Alcantára, one of the 'Inca trails' that criss-crossed the country.

A PROFITABLE DYNASTIC CRISIS

When Pizarro arrived in Peru, two sons of the Inca Emperor Huayna Capac (died in 1528) were arguing over who would inherit the empire from their father. In their quest for power, Huáscar (1503-1532) was supported by the nobility of Cuzco, which enabled him to take his father's throne, while his half-brother Atahualpa (c. 1500-1533) was supported by the nobility of Quito. In 1532, Atahualpa seized the imperial throne of Cuzco after a civil war in which he killed his brother. Pizarro took advantage of this dynastic crisis to succeed on several different levels and assert his power over local populations.

PIZARRO AGAINST THE INCAS: FROM CAJAMARCA TO AN EXECUTION

Advancing towards the south, Pizarro and his men met many Native Peruvians. Local chiefs offered them shelter and food in return for peace and mutual respect. In the valley of the Piura River, Pizarro decided to build a town that would act as a base when they climbed the nearby mountain range, on the land owned by the Native Peruvian chief of Tangarará and the riverbanks. The town, named San Miguel de Piura, was founded on 15 August 1532.

Hernando de Soto, sent to scout in the mountains, reached Cajas, followed by Huancabamba, whose riches were beyond the conquistadors' wildest dreams. After meeting and welcoming Atahualpa's messenger, and after an exchange of gifts as a token of friendship and respect, he informed Pizarro of his discovery. While they waited for a meeting with the Inca, the Spaniards continued to advance towards the south in autumn 1532. After crossing the Sechura Desert, they reached the modern-day towns of Olmos, Motupe and Jayanca, where Native Peruvian villages were settled. Pizarro was perceptive and understood the stakes of the situation: civil war was raging across the country and Atahualpa, in charge of an army of several thousand men, only increased the terror. After a seven-month expedition, Pizarro decided to change course, cross the Andes and go to meet the emperor. The Inca was curious and sent supplies and gifts to them throughout their journey. In reality, this was a way of getting his men near to Pizarro to evaluate his troops and their state. The meeting took place in Cajamarca, at around 2800 metres above sea level, on 16 November 1532.

Just as wary as the Inca, Pizarro did not have the peaceful intentions that he wanted to demonstrate: thanks to the indications provided by de Soto and Hernando Pizarro, he devised a strategy to capture the Inca. According to literary tradition, the troops on both sides were ready to attack and destroy every last enemy soldier. The trigger of the attack was the affront – judged thus by the Spaniards –to the Dominican Vicente de Valverde (1498-1541), when he presented a Bible to the Inca who, through contempt or ignorance, threw it to the ground. Pizarro then gave the signal to attack. Immediately, Spanish troops rushed at the Native Peruvians, whom they destroyed. Thanks to the element of surprise, there were hundreds of injured Native Peruvians, the Inca was taken prisoner and his riches were pillaged. According to one historian, the plunder was as high as 80 000 gold pesos, 7000 silver marks and 7 marks (around 10 kg) of emeralds.

The seizure of Atahualpa at Cajamarca, engraving by Pierre Duflos, between 1760 and 1810.

Atahualpa's fate was now in Pizarro's hands. His ambition and the extreme greed that motivated the Spanish side led him to negotiate the life of the emperor against a ransom. The Inca offered to fill an entire room with gold and two others with silver from across the empire, mainly from the capital, Cuzco, or the main sanctuary, Pachacamac, in 40 days. During his captivity, Atahualpa, in close contact with his supporters, managed to have his brother Huascár, who was being held prisoner in Cuzco, assassinated in order to avoid any negotiation with the Spaniards at his expense.

On 12 April 1533, Diego de Almagro, returning from Panama, arrived in Cajamarca with reinforcements, to compete with his associate and, above all, to lead a new conquest to the north – a zone not yet explored by Pizarro. The division of the spoils, which took place on 17 and 18 June, between Pizarro, de Soto and Benalcázar's men and the new arrivals stoked fresh tensions among the Spaniards: faced with an unequal division, Almagro's men felt wronged. Of the 168 people involved, the Pizarro brothers alone received 11% of the plunder. In summer, Hernando Pizarro was sent to the monarchy to show them the treasures that had been disco-vered and hope to rally new participants to the conquest of Peru.

While tensions flared over the Spaniards' spoils, the Native Peruvians hiding in the area around Cajamarca were trying to organise an operation to free the emperor. But, aware of the risks of a native attack and determined to assert Spanish supremacy over local populations, Pizarro sealed the Inca's fate on 26 July. Accused of the murder of Huascár and the betrayal of the Spaniards, he was condemned to death by burning at the stake in the main square of Cajamarca. He requested baptism in extremis, which allowed him to commute his sentence and be put to death by hanging. In order to win the support of the indigenous elite, Pizarro appointed a new Inca emperor, the young Túpac Huallpa (died in 1533), son of Huayna Cápac, and therefore Atahualpa and Huascár's half-brother. Supported by the Cuzco nobility, he was placed under Pizarro's protection as soon as he arrived. In reality, he was a puppet emperor of Pizarro.

THE END OF THE CONQUEST

Before setting off across the Andes to reach Cuzco, Pizarro put Benalcazár in charge of San Miguel de Piura, forcing one of his best but least accommodating lieutenants to assume the management of the city, of which the port was the only point of disembarkation from the isthmus of Panama, and above all to lead the conquest of the north, overtaking the new arrivals in search of territories and riches. For three months, progress across the Andes mountain range, following the Inca trail, went smoothly: despite occasionally difficult conditions, Pizarro only met with very little resistance from the Native Peruvians. The riches therefore started to pile up. However, while on the exploration, Túpac Huallpa contracted cholera. While Hernando de Soto had paved the way by occasionally attacking indigenous populations, not hesitating to resort to force during increasingly frequent conflicts, Pizarro entered the town of Cuzco, which was completely deserted, on 14 November 1533. The *Coricancha* ('sun house') temple, the main place of worship, was pillaged for its gold and the royal sanctuary was desecrated.

Anxious to gain the support of the Cuzco aristocracy, Pizarro appointed Manco Cápac (also known as Manco Inca or

Manca Inca Yupanqui, died in 1545), Túpac Huallpa's brother, as emperor. On 23 March 1534, Pizarro founded a Spanish town on the site of the former capital, rid it of its indigenous appearance, planted crosses and made one of the buildings into the main church. This was the second town founded by the Spaniards, over 1300 miles away from the first one (San Miguel). While the conquest of the south seemed well underway, Pizarro was aware of the hostility of the Native Peruvians led by Quizquiz, one of Atahualpa's generals who, since the trap in Cajamarca, had been leading the resistance. On the Spanish side, problems increased and Pizarro had to deal with Almagro and Benalcázar's ambitions, the often uncontrollable energy of Hernando de Soto and the imminent arrival of new hopefuls brought to Quito by Alvarado.

In April 1534, the foundation of the new town of Jauja from nothing allowed them to establish easy access to the coast. Pizarro intended to make it the new capital of colonial Peru. From there, he travelled down along the coast to reach an oasis where Lima would later be founded, followed by Pachacamac, Lurín, Mala, Lunahuana and eventually Chincha, which he had heard so much about during his first voyage and where his authority had been recognised by the monarchy in 1529.

IMPACT

THE PIZARROS' CONTROL: TENSION AND GREED

Pizarro's success in Peru paved the way for many conquistadors. From 1533, ships from Nicaragua brought claimants to the fortune in South America. The wealth of the Inca treasures and the news of Pizarro's success in fact encouraged many other Spaniards to try their luck. Although new expeditions were launched, Peru's main discoverer and his troops were never matched. When the expedition led by Alvarado in 1534 (a dozen ships, 450 soldiers and 2000 Native Peruvians and slaves) headed towards the region of Quito, Pizarro's lieutenant, Benalcázar, intervened. Almagro, who hurried to the scene, negotiated and bought all the ships and men for the impressive sum of 100 000 ducats. Aware that he could only exist outside of the bubble of Pizarro's power, Benalcázar then decided to become independent and, with a few other men, left to conquer the province of Popayán (in the south of modern-day Colombia).

The dominance of Pizarro and those close to him across the territory was met with fierce opposition. On the one hand, the arrogance and greed of the Pizarro brothers created additional tension with the Native Peruvians, but also with the Spaniards. Using terror to assert their authority and conducting many acts of violence and extortion, they used violence excessively, particularly in Cuzco where they treated Manco Cápac without any respect, held him prisoner and kept him chained up, and constantly humiliated him. However, the Inca managed to escape them, hiding in the mountains in Ollantaytambo. Guerrilla warfare then broke out. From April to May 1536, during the siege of Cuzco by the Native Peruvians, Juan Pizarro was fatally wounded during a violent clash. In August 1536, Lima was attacked, but without their leader, Titu Yupanqui, who was killed in the fight, the Native Peruvian armies eventually retreated. While, for his part, Pizarro continued his project of conquest and assertion of his power thanks to a policy of founding new towns – such as Lima (named Ciudad de los Reyes) on 18 January 1535 – internal tensions increased on the Spanish side. A few months earlier, in May 1534, Hernando Pizarro had obtained the new *Capitulación* from the king, which stipulated the division of new territories between Pizarro and Almagro. Unlike the one in 1529, Almagro was not left out this time. Appointed Governor of New Toledo – an area that could be fully conquered – he argued with his associate about Cuzco and its riches. During the negotiations that recognised Pizarro's power over the former Inca capital, the latter agreed to help Almagro to launch the expedition to New Toledo (in the south, near Chile), which began on 12 June 1535. But the expedition was a failure: no treasure comparable to those of the Incas was found. In February 1537, Almagro decided to return and claim what he believed he was owed, the town of Cuzco. As part of his plan to oust the Pizarros, he tried in vain to make Manco Cápac an associate of his. Despite the negotiations led by Hernando Pizarro, Almagro remained unmoving. He entered the town in April 1537, occupied it and had Pizarro's brothers (Hernando and Gonzalo) arrested. Francisco Pizarro, who was in Lima at the time, hurried back with his troops and went to negotiate his brothers' release in person. In exchange for a hefty ransom and homage paid to Almagro, Hernando and Gonzalo were released.

The Battle of Las Salinas and the death of Almagro

This insult to Pizarro was unbearable. When he returned to Lima, he left Hernando in charge of the expedition to punish Almagro. On 6 April 1538, in Las Salinas, a battle recognised the victory of the Pizarros' 700 men against Almagro's chaotic troops. Their leader was arrested and charged with treason against the Spanish monarchy. During the trial, in which he hoped to benefit from his longstanding friendship with the governor, Almagro was sentenced to death and beheaded on 8 July 1538.

Almagro's execution marked a decisive turning point, both in the history of Peru and Pizarro's personal history. All hopefuls for power had been ousted, and nothing was now stopping his family from having full control over the new territories. From then on, Francisco Pizarro's objectives were to create peace in the area, to found more towns, to put an end to the hostility of the Native Peruvians, whose leader, Manco Cápac, had retreated to Vilcabamba, and finally to lead a new expedition to the south (towards modern-day Bolivia). The monarchy granted him the title of marquis in October 1537, something that was rather exceptional for a conquistador – only Cortés had received the same honour. Free to choose his territory, Pizarro chose the region of

Atabillos (north of Lima), a region that was not very well-known and as of yet unexplored.

At the end of the 1530s, the power of the Pizarro family was based on the accumulation of wealth throughout the conquest, tax collection across their territories, mining activities and trade routes set up from Peru to Spain.

A VIOLENT DEATH WITH DECISIVE CONSEQUENCES

In 1540, new problems arose: a revolt by the Native Peruvians was violently repressed. The ancient tribes of Chili, poor and resentful, found in Almagro's son a leader for the resistance that was forming. Born in around 1520, Diego de Almagro II, known as *el Mozo* (the lad), exiled to Lima following the death of his father, assumed the leadership of a conspiracy to assassinate Pizarro. Pizarro was warned, but paid little attention. On 26 June 1541, under the orders of Juan de Rada (died in 1541), a former captain under Cortés and a member of Almagro's party, 12 men arrived to assassinate him. Pizarro and his brother, Martín de Alcantára, were violently attacked.

Pizarro's assassination.

His death would have direct repercussions. Firstly, a full-scale witch hunt was launched: while Pizarro's children were protected, his men were killed by Almagro's supporters or Native Peruvians. A civil war broke out between the conquistadors, leading to the crucial intervention of the monarchy, which sent a governor and decreed a series of laws intended for America (20 November 1542). With Pizarro's death, the era of the great conquistadors came to an end, in favour of necessarily stricter interventionism and control on the part of the monarchy, which suppressed the revolt led by Gonzalo Pizarro in 1544.

NEW WORLD, NEW KNOWLEDGE

From a geographical point of view, all the maritime maps dating from before 1520 limited their representation of the Americas to the east coast (from north to south). The acquisition of new knowledge, thanks in particular to the expedition led by Magellan (and the strait crossed in 1520), complemented by expeditions in the following years, including that of Pizarro and his followers, allowed new maps to be drawn up.

One notable example of this is one of the very first maps, which is in fact the largest portolan chart (marine map illustrating the ports, seabeds and tides of a part of the world) in existence. It was drawn up by the Portuguese cartographer Andreas Homem in 1559 and is known as the *Universa ac navigabilis totius terrarium orbis descriptio*, featuring South America in its entirety – the contours of the southern side noticeably less distinct – and the full geography of Peru and the west coast.

SUMMARY

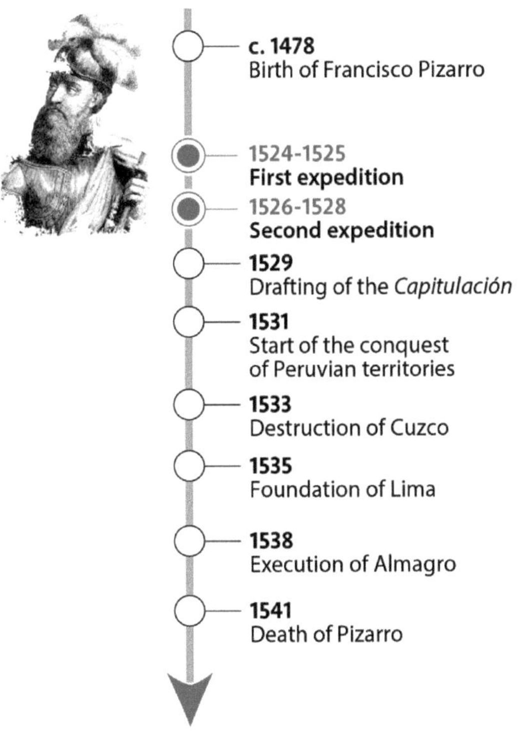

Francisco Pizarro © **50MINUTES**.com

- Pizarro was one of the most ambitious conquistadors of his generation. Keen for recognition, he did not hesitate to make his men rise to all the challenges necessary to accomplishing his mission: discovering, conquering and taking over a new area, as well as acquiring wealth.

- After taking part in several expeditions to Central America, he became an associate of Diego de Almagro and the monk Hernando de Luque in the *Empresa del Levante.*
- After two exploration expeditions that cost many lives and a great deal of money, empowered by the *Capitulación* granted by the Spanish monarchy, Pizarro set off to conquer Peruvian territories in 1531. He thus discovered the wealth of the Inca Empire. But his conquest was not without conflicts with the local population, and tensions within the Spanish group increased.
- Taking advantage of the bloody family war between the descendants of the Inca Huanya Cápac, Pizarro managed to capture Atahualpa, the last Inca Emperor, during an ambush in Cajamarca in November 1532. After demanding a ransom in exchange for his life, he had him executed in July 1533.
- The conquest led by Pizarro was not a peaceful one: massacres, pillages and violence were typical of the actions of the governor's men and brothers. On 14 November 1533, after crossing the Andes, Pizarro reached the old Inca capital, Cuzco, which his men destroyed, motivated entirely by greed. The *Coricancha*, a religious centre that symbolised Inca power, was ransacked and pillaged. In under three years, Pizarro demolished the Inca Empire, depriving it of its strength, its wealth, its roots and its customs.
- As part of his ambition to establish a new map of the country, Pizarro founded many towns, some from nothing and some on ancient Inca sites that he renamed. On 18 January 1535, he gave the country a new capital, Ciudad

de los Reyes (Lima).

- Throughout the conquest, greed, violence, jealousy and disappointment caused his associate Almagro and some of the troops to oppose the Pizarro brothers. The conflicts were violent, and there were many victims, including Almagro, who was executed in 1538.
- After eliminating any hopefuls for power on the Spanish side, and killing or chasing out the Native Peruvian chiefs, Pizarro completed the conquest and launched new expeditions towards the south while new arrivals seized the border areas.
- Rivalries between the Spanish clans eventually got the better of Pizarro, who was killed in June 1541 during an attack carried out by Almagro's followers, led by his son, Diego Almagro II, *el Mozo*.
- When Pizarro died, a whole era died with him: that of the great conquistadors, which came to an end. From now on, the Spanish monarchy would monitor conquered territories more closely, adopting a resolutely interventionist policy.

We want to hear from you!
Leave a comment on your online library
and share your favourite books on social media!

FIND OUT MORE

BIBLIOGRAPHY

- Bénat-Tachot, L. and Lavallé, B. (2005) *L'Amérique de Charles Quint.* Bordeaux: Presses universitaires de Bordeaux.
- BNF. (No date) *L'Âge d'or des cartes marines.* [Online]. [Accessed 30 September 2009]. Available from: <http://expositions.bnf.fr/marine/index.htm>
- Chaunu, P. (1995) *Conquête et exploitation des nouveaux mondes.* Paris: PUF.
- Cieza de León, P. (1979) *Descubrimiento y conquista del Perú.* Rome: Éditions Francesca Cantu.
- Hoffmann, C., Richard, H. and Vagnon, E. (2012) *L'âge d'or des cartes marines. Quand l'Europe découvrait le monde.* Paris: Seuil/Bibliothèque nationale de France.
- De Jerez, F. (1982) *La Conquête du Pérou.* Paris: A.-M. Métailié.
- De La Hoz, P. S. (1987) Relation pour S.M. de ce qui arriva pendant la conquête et la pacification de ces provinces de la Nouvelle-Castille et de la qualité de la terre, après que le capitaine Hernando Pizarro s'en alla porter à S.M. la relation de la victoire de Caxamalca et de la capture du cacique Atabalipa. In F. Carrillo, ed. *Cartas y cronistas del descubrimiento y la conquista.* Lima: Éditorial Horizonte.
- Lavallé, B. (2004) *Francisco Pizarro, conquistador de l'extrême.* Paris: Éditions Payot et Rivages.
- Lockhart, J. (1987) *Los de Cajamarca, un estudio social y biográfico de los primeros conquistadores del Perú,* vol. 2.

Lima: Milla Batres.
- De Mena, C. (1987) Conquista del Peru illamada la Nueva Castilla. In: F. Carrillo, ed. *Cartas y cronistas del descubrimiento y la conquista.* Lima: Éditorial Horizonte.
- Pizarro, P. (2012) *An Account of the Conquest of Peru.* London: Forgotten Books.

ADDITIONAL SOURCES

- Hemming, J. (2003) *The Conquest of the Incas.* New York: Mariner Books.
- MacQuarrie, K. (2008) *The Last Days of the Incas.* New York: Simon and Schuster.
- Stirling, S. (2005) *Pizarro: Conqueror of the Inca.* Stroud: Sutton Publishing Limited.

ICONOGRAPHIC SOURCES

- Portrait of Francisco Pizarro. Royalty-free reproduction picture.
- *The seizure of Atahualpa at Cajamarca,* engraving by Pierre Duflos, between 1760 and 1810. Royalty-free reproduction picture.
- Pizarro's assassination. Royalty-free reproduction picture.

IMPROVE YOUR GENERAL KNOWLEDGE

IN A BLINK OF AN EYE !

www.50minutes.com